ABRAHAM LINCOLN
THE BOY • THE MAN
by Lloyd Ostendorf

Using photographs and drawings, LLoyd Ostendorf brings to life all the well-known episodes, and some less well-known, that occurred during the fifty-six years of Lincoln's life. The day he fell into Knob Creek and nearly drowned, his experience taking cargo down the Mississippi to New Orleans on a flatboat, and the plot to assassinate him as he and his party made their way to Washington for the first inauguration may be less familiar to us than Lincoln doing long division on the wooden fire shovel. Skillfully and with the most careful attention to detail, Lloyd Ostendorf recreates these and one hundred and fifty other events.

The brief text supplements the illustrations and tells the facts about each of the pictures. The authentic photographs, together with the action drawings, provide the young reader with an accurate and fascinating panorama of the life history of one of our greatest Americans. OVER 225 drawings and photographs picturing the full life story of LINCOLN.

AUTHOR and ARTIST Lloyd Ostendorf is a gifted artist and photographer. Lincolniana has been his hobby for over 50 years. The list of historical societies to which he belongs goes on and on, as does the list of publications to which he has contributed. Photographs from his large Civil War collection appear in the American Heritage PICTURE HISTORY OF THE CIVIL WAR. Since his early teens he has been fascinated by Lincoln, and as he says, "A quarter of a century of collecting his pictures, and drawing his likeness for fun and for publication was bound to result some day in a book. This is it."

"*Herewith is a little sketch . . . There is not much of it, for the reason, I suppose, that there is not much of me. If anything be made out of it, I wish it to be modest, and not go beyond the material. . . .*"

Yours very truly,
A. LINCOLN

(From a letter to J. W. Fell, December 20, 1859)

ABRAHAM

LINCOLN

THE BOY THE MAN

BY LLOYD OSTENDORF

illustrated by the author

Publisher:
Phillip H. Wagner
Wagner Office Systems
2800-2 South Sixth Street
Springfield, IL 62703
(217) 523-3692

To My Children,

Dan, Tom, and Roxanne

CONTENTS

The log cabin in which Lincoln is said to have been born, before it was placed in the Memorial Building at the Abraham Lincoln National Historical Park near Hodgenville, Kentucky.

A HUMBLE BIRTH . . . 1809

Abraham Lincoln was born February 12, 1809, in a log cabin near Hodgenville, Kentucky. His mother, Nancy, proudly showed her infant son to his sister Sarah and his cousin Dennis Hanks.

Author's collection

The Boundary Oak. The aged white oak tree on the boundary line of the Lincoln farm is believed to be about 400 years old.

AT THE LINCOLN FARM
ON NOLIN CREEK . . . 1810

Near the great white oak, the ancient boundary tree on the land where Abraham Lincoln was born, Mrs. Thomas Lincoln would gently rock her infant son Abe while she chatted with his little sister Sarah.

12

LITTLE ABRAHAM, THE TAG-ALONG . . . 1811

Dressed in a linsey-woolsey shirt, two-year-old Abe would follow his sister as she carried a pail of fresh water from the rock spring not far from their cabin on the Sinking Spring farm.

LITTLE ABE MET A SOLDIER . . . 1812

When Abraham Lincoln was asked if he remembered anything about the War of 1812 with Great Britain, he replied, telling of a happening when he was four:

"I had been fishing one day and caught a little fish which I was taking home. I met a soldier on the road, and, having been always told at home that we must be kind to the soldiers, I gave him my fish."

14

L. M. U. collection

The big corn field
on the Knob Creek farm

CHORES ON THE KENTUCKY FARM . . . 1813

Abraham Lincoln remembered his boyhood home in Kentucky very well, and that one of his first chores was to plant the pumpkin seeds. "Sometimes when there came a big rain in the hills the water would come down through the gorges . . . I dropped two seeds in every other hill and every other row . . .

"One time the rain from the hills came down and washed corn and pumpkin seeds clear off the field."

15

The Knob Creek farm cabin as it can be seen today

A PRESENT FROM HIS FATHER . . . 1814

At a sale at Thomas Hill's place on July 19, 1814, Thomas Lincoln bought, for eight and one-third cents, a homemade "truck wagon" for his son. This toy must have really delighted five-year-old Abraham, who had very few playthings in that pioneer country.

OFF TO ABC SCHOOL IN THE FALL OF 1815 . . .

Abraham eagerly marched off to his first day at school with his sister
Sarah and their dog Honey. The log school, taught by schoolmaster
Zachariah Riney, was about two miles northeast of the Lincoln home.

17

ABE'S DOG AND THE WILDCAT . . . 1815

One day six-year-old Abe Lincoln went into the woods with an older friend, Austin Gollaher, who was going to hunt. Abe's hound dog, Honey, bounding on ahead, ran into a wildcat. Soon a fight was on, and the fur flew. Young Abe jumped up and down excitedly as he shouted for Austin to shoot the cat. Before Austin could do so the tussle ended, the wildcat going one way and Honey going the other, minus a few hairs. Said young Abe, "I thought that wildcat was going to skin Honey alive!"

18

Knob Creek

Philip Van Doren Stern

THE DAY ABE FELL IN KNOB CREEK . . . 1816

Shortly before the Lincoln family moved from Kentucky, young Abe and Austin spent a day along Knob Creek. The water was high from recent rains. Abe wanted to cross the creek on a log footbridge to search for a flock of wild partridge he had seen there the day before. While he was working his way across the foot-log, he fell in. He could not swim, and began to thrash around. Austin looked for a stick he could hold out to Abe.

Austin found a long sycamore limb and held it out for Abe to catch hold, but Abe had nearly drowned before Austin could pull him to safety. The boys promised to keep the event a secret to avoid a spanking from their parents. Years later Austin told the story many times.

19

CHILD OF THE WILDERNESS ... 1816

Abraham received only a little real education in ABC schools, as they were called. But what he learned from his mother and from the outdoor wilderness gave him a wealth of useful knowledge.

With his faithful dog, Abe would watch the many creatures of the forest not far from the cabin on Knob Creek. He learned the names of the trees and plants in the woods, as well as the lessons nature taught to those who lived close to it.

LEAVING "OLD KENTUCKY" . . . 1816

Abe took one last look at the Knob Creek farm, while from her seat in the wagon Sarah thought about the life they were leaving behind and the new one they would find in the state of Indiana. A short while before, with their mother, they had paid a last visit to the Redmon cemetery, to the grave of their baby brother, Tommy Lincoln, who had died at the age of three; that was one reason they did not want to leave Kentucky. But when Father Tom Lincoln had so much trouble over the ownership of his farms, and saw the evils of slavery taking a greater hold on the state, he decided to try to make a new start in Indiana— a free state.

THE YOUNG WOODSMAN . . .
DECEMBER, 1816

Abe's father taught him how to use an ax at an early age, and he did his full share of work when everyone helped to build a new home in the Indiana wilderness.

Neighbors helped Tom Lincoln lay up the log walls of the cabin. Abe and Sarah helped to mix the "wattle and daub" mortar that was made with clay and grass and used for filling between the logs. Abraham's growing years, from boyhood to manhood, were spent in Indiana.

22

ABE SHOT A WILD TURKEY . . .
FEBRUARY, 1817

Abe had an early start as a hunter in Indiana, but he never became very skillful, even though Spencer County was a wild region, with many bears and other wild animals still in the woods.

A flock of wild turkeys approached the new cabin one day. Abe's father was not at home, so Abe asked his mother if he could take his father's gun and shoot at the large birds through the crack between the logs. Permission granted, he shot and killed one of them. Abe was not so happy about his marksmanship as he was pleased by the beauty of the great bird he had brought down.

(*Inset*) Wild turkeys. The wild gobblers in America have smaller heads, larger eyes, and a more streamlined body than tame birds.

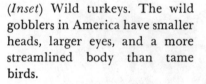

LITTLE ABE, THE PENMAN . . . 1817

Many of the pioneer settlers learned that young Abe Lincoln had unusual talents for his age. He could read and write, while many older people could barely write their own names. Abraham's skill as a penman was often put to use. He wrote letters for his family and friends. The settlers thought him very wise and well educated.

STUDYING BY FIRELIGHT . . . 1817

Abe would write and figure on any scraps of paper he could find, and when he had no more paper, he wrote with charcoal sticks on the wooden fire-shovel and other objects. Among the few books he studied were Dilworth's Spelling-book and the family Bible.

THE CUSTOM ON THE SABBATH . . . 1817

Seldom was there a chance for the Lincolns to attend a religious service in their neighborhood on the Sabbath. So a portion of the day of rest was spent in telling stories from the Bible. When Sarah and Abe learned to read they took their turns in the duty of Sunday reading.

"RAISED TO FARM LABOR . . ." 1817

Thomas Lincoln taught his son Abraham the pioneer woodcrafts as well as farm work. At an early age little Abe learned the art of making barn shakes from a bolt of cedar. His father, an accomplished carpenter and cabinetmaker, had little chance to work at his trade in the wilderness, but he could demonstrate his skill in working with wood— the use of the mall for hammering and the froe for splitting—in forming shingles from a short log.

SARAH WAS HELPFUL

WITH HOUSEHOLD CHORES . . .

Abe's older sister Sarah was useful in the cabin at the age of ten—cooking, cleaning, and helping to keep the simple clothing in good order were some of her tasks. When not assisting her mother she was a close friend to her brother, and probably helped him with his meager schoolwork, too.

Philip Van Doren Stern

Site of Nancy Hanks Lincoln's grave on a wooded knoll a quarter of a mile from the Lincoln cabin home in Spencer County, Indiana. (A headstone with Nancy Lincoln's initials has been painted into the photograph.)

GRIM DAYS FOR THE LINCOLN CHILDREN . . . 1818

Abraham was only nine when his mother died from the milk sickness in 1818. After making a thoughtful visit to their mother's lonely grave, Sarah and her brother slowly descended the gentle slope as the trees watched silently.

29

THE LONELY LITTLE LINCOLN GIRL . . .

1818

Poor little Sarah Lincoln did the cabin chores and cooking as best she could for an eleven-year-old. She felt the loss of her mother deeply, and there were no loving aunts or relatives to console her.

Cousin Dennis Hanks and Abe caught a baby coon and a turtle for her—to try to cheer her up—but most of the time she would just sit by the fire and cry.

30

"KICKED BY A HORSE,
AND APPARENTLY KILLED . . ." 1818

Noah Gordon's horse-powered gristmill was less than two miles from
the Lincolns' Indiana cabin. Abe, watching the slow process as he
waited for those ahead of him to get their grain ground, once remarked that "his dog could eat the meal as fast as the mill could
grind it." When his turn came one day, Abe hitched his horse to the
beam and urged the old mare along with a switch. But she didn't like
being hurried, and when Abe tried to hasten her once too often, he
received a swift kick in the head. Poor Abe, in a coma for a time, was
almost given up as dead. Happily, the nine-year-old boy finally recovered from his serious accident.

A NEW MOTHER
FOR THE INDIANA ORPHANS . . . 1819

It was more than a year after the death of Nancy Hanks Lincoln that Thomas Lincoln went back to Kentucky to seek a wife and mother for his children.

He married Sally Bush Johnston, a widow with three children—Elizabeth, John D., and Matilda—and brought them all back to the Indiana home in the wilderness.

The Lincoln children and Dennis Hanks, who was nearly grown, had gotten along for weeks by themselves, so it was with mixed emotions that the forlorn Lincoln children greeted their handsome and affectionate stepmother the day she arrived.

ABE LINCOLN—HOOSIER BOY . . . 1819

Young Abe in Indiana, large for his age, might have looked something like this to his friends and neighbors in the Hoosier State where he grew up. The settlers had noticed this boy who was raised on the farm, and they knew his skill with an ax; but they were more amazed at his early search for knowledge and his liking for books. They remembered seeing him seated on a fence, silently reading and dreaming.

SMALL ACORNS INTO
GREAT OAK TREES GROW . . . 1819

Though Lincoln practiced the art of public speaking as a boy, he never became very famous as an orator. But the strength of the words he spoke later in life did become important for all Americans.

As a boy he could repeat word for word the sermon heard at a meeting and imitate the way the preacher had given it. And at school he once mounted a stump to recite an essay he had composed on cruelty to animals. Later, farm laborers in the field would stop their work to hear young Lincoln's lectures, known for their strength, clarity, and humor. When he was twenty-one his friends said he could "beat to death" any other backwoods speaker. Though never a polished orator, he developed an able, logical way of speaking.

A BOYHOOD CHORE—
TO THE MILL ON HORSEBACK . . . 1819

Lincoln once said that riding horseback to the gristmill gave him his
greatest boyhood pleasure. With his
grain sacks filled, Abe would wave to
his friends at the mill and head home-
ward, having spent several delightful
hours of newsy gossip and story swap-
ping.

PIONEER "BLAB" SCHOOL . . . 1820

For about three months Abe Lincoln attended a "blab" school kept by Andrew Crawford. The log schoolhouse was about a mile and a half from the Lincoln home in the Little Pigeon Creek community in Spencer County, Indiana.

Here everyone recited his lessons out loud, at the same time—an old method of teaching. The pupils also had spelling matches and learned etiquette, along with their "readin', writin', and cipherin'."

THE DILEMMA OF
THE HORNS . . . 1820

A buck's head was mounted on the schoolhouse wall. Since he was so tall for his age, Abe's friends dared him to jump up and touch the buck's horns. He did jump up and hung on the antlers, but one side broke from his weight.

When the schoolmaster arrived he asked who broke the deer's horn.

"I did it," answered Lincoln promptly, "I wouldn't have done it if I thought it would break." Because of his honesty Abe was not punished, and he also earned a nickname from his friends, "Honest Abe."

THOMAS LINCOLN— INDUSTRIOUS PIONEER . . . 1820

Tom Lincoln, Abraham's father, has often been unfairly called "a lazy, shiftless man. . . ." Actually he was a hard-working, God-fearing pioneer. He was a talented carpenter, skilled with the ax and other tools, and he taught his son to use them, too. He worked as a boat builder, farmer, and contractor, and his skill as a cabinet-maker is proven by the half dozen or so of his cupboards still in existence. He built cabins, mills, wagons, wheels, and furniture between farming chores, and provided for his family as well as other settlers in the Indiana wilderness did.

THE PIGEON CREEK CHURCH—LOG HOUSE OF WORSHIP . . . 1822

Thomas Lincoln had been chosen by the church committee to direct the building of the Little Pigeon Meetinghouse. He did some of the actual work as well; he built the pulpit and window casings and did other cabinet work. Abraham was proud to assist his father, the boss carpenter on the job.

The Lincoln family is shown returning from services. Thomas Lincoln was a trustee of the Little Pigeon Church.

O. V. Brown

AN OLD INDIANA ELM
THAT "KNEW" THE LINCOLNS . . . 1820

A stately old elm tree, a stone's throw behind the Lincoln cabin in
Indiana, was for a long time the only living link in the Hoosier State
with the Lincoln family. After about 400 years of life, the tree, king
of the forest, died in 1959, the 150th anniversary of Lincoln's birth,
and the farm where Abe grew up lost its living landmark.

38

ABE GREW IN BOOK KNOWLEDGE
AND HORSE SENSE . . . 1823

In the solitude of the woods, hills, and fields, Abe Lincoln would pause from his daily work to rest and read.

Whether he lay in the grass in the shade of a tree, or perched atop a rail fence with book in hand, the outdoor wilderness was his classroom. In nature's quiet surroundings Abe lost no opportunity to read and think; indeed, he often took extra time to think and study when work awaited!

"ABRAHAM LINCOLN
HIS HAND AND PEN . . ." 1825

Young Lincoln attended Azel W. Dorsey's school in Spencer County, Indiana. Abraham kept a copybook from 1824 to 1826 and in it wrote sums from his studies in arithmetic. At times he would write down a few lines of verse. An example of his schoolboy doggerel can be seen here, on one of the pages of his exercise book—"Abraham Lincoln his hand and pen, he will be good but God knows when."

Library of Congress

A book Lincoln read

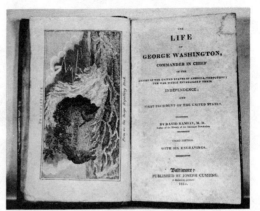

THREE DAYS' LABOR FOR A BOOK . . . 1827

So strong was young Lincoln's desire for self-education and knowledge that it is said he borrowed and read every book he could get his hands on—every book within fifty miles of his Indiana home.

From his neighbor, Josiah Crawford, he borrowed David Ramsey's *Life of George Washington*. By accident, rain badly damaged the book one night. Honest young Abe confessed to Mr. Crawford what had happened to his book, and told him he had no money to pay for it but offered to work out the book's value. Mr. Crawford accepted, and Abe pulled fodder in Crawford's cornfield for several days and became the proud owner of the book.

41

ABE'S LITTLE PRANK . . . 1827

Not long after the Lincoln cabin ceiling had been whitewashed, Abe thought up a stunt to tease his mother. A couple of young boys were wading in a mud puddle outside near the horse trough. Abe took the muddy-footed boys inside, picked one of them up, and carried him upside down across the room, letting the youngster track his footprints on the ceiling.

Then they waited for Mother Lincoln to come in. When she saw the practical joke, she burst into laughter. The fun over, Abe cleaned the ceiling.

ABE EARNS HIS FIRST DOLLAR . . . 1827

When Abe was in his late teens he worked for a time at ferrying passengers across Anderson Creek, near where it flowed into the Ohio River. One day two gentlemen came down to the river landing where Abe had his homemade boat. They had luggage with them, and they wanted to catch a river packet waiting in midstream. They hired Abe, who was glad for a chance to earn something, to take them to the steamer. After Abe helped the men and their trunks safely aboard, each tossed a silver half dollar into his boat. Abe could scarcely believe that he had earned a dollar in less than a day, and the incident made him more hopeful and confident from that time on.

Two sides of silver half dollar, 1827

ABE—A GOOD SAMARITAN . . . 1827

One cold night, as Lincoln and his friend Dave Turnham were walking along a road, they came upon the body of a man lying near a mud puddle. They soon recognized him as a respectable member of the Indiana community. He was hopelessly drunk, and they could not wake him. Turnham left for home, saying the man should lie in the bed he had made for himself, but Abe thought he might freeze to death during the cold night and decided to help him. Taking the unconscious man in his long arms, Abe carried him a great distance to the house of his cousin, Dennis Hanks, where he was revived. Later the man said that Abe's merciful deed had saved his life.

ABE LOSES HIS ONLY SISTER . . . 1828

Abraham's sister Sarah, who was two years older than he was, had married Aaron Grigsby. When she died in childbirth a year and a half later, Aaron ran a quarter of a mile to Reuben Grigsby's place to tell Abe. He found Abe in the smokehouse doing carpentry work. When he heard the shocking news, Abe sat down in the doorway and cried. Now he was more alone in the world than ever.

"THE THINGS I WANT TO KNOW
ARE IN BOOKS . . ." 1828

As the fireside was Lincoln's study by night, the shade of the white oak was his classroom by day. Abe had always read while resting from his farm labors, and now that he was almost grown he began to think about the ideas he got from books. He knew the time had come for him to leave farm work behind and pursue greater things. Only by learning more from books could he ever hope to make his dreams of the future come true.

ABE'S FIRST TRIP
TO NEW ORLEANS . . . 1828

In 1828, when Lincoln was nineteen, a wealthy merchant, James Gentry, hired him to help his son Allen take a flatboat of produce down the Mississippi on a trading trip. Allen had taken the 1,222-mile trip with his father several times before, so he was the captain and Abe the deck hand. They sold the load of produce along the way, and when they reached New Orleans they sold the flatboat for its lumber and returned home upriver by steamboat. The whole trip took about three months.

Elihu Stout Print Shop Memorial, Vincennes, Ind.

Author's collection

LINCOLN SEES HIS FIRST
PRINTING PRESS . . . MARCH, 1830

The Lincolns decided to move farther west. On the way from Indiana to Illinois in March, 1830, they stopped at Vincennes for a day. There, twenty-one-year-old Abraham visited editor Elihu Stout's newspaper, *The Western Sun,* and was fascinated to see a printing press for the first time.

THE VINCENNES VISITORS
SEE THE CATHEDRAL . . . MARCH, 1830

Thirteen members of the Lincoln family made the journey from Spencer County, Indiana, to Macon County, Illinois—Thomas Lincoln and wife Sarah, Abraham, John D. Johnston, Dennis Hanks and his wife and four children, and John Hall and his wife and infant son. While in Vincennes, before they crossed the Wabash River and headed west, they passed the old Cathedral, which was begun in 1824, and which can be seen today in all its stately beauty.

Lincoln Monument, Vincennes,
Indiana, Nellie V. Walker,
sculptress

WHERE LINCOLN
CROSSED THE WABASH . . . MARCH, 1830

It was a cold day in March, 1830, when the Lincoln party crossed the
ice-covered Wabash River, leaving Indiana to enter the state of Illinois.
Abe's favorite dog, jumped out of the ox-drawn wagon onto the thin
ice, and broke through. Abe jumped into icy water up to his waist to
rescue his dog.

THE RAIL-SPLITTER AT WORK . . . 1830

During the presidential campaign of 1860 Abe Lincoln became known as the "Rail-splitter Candidate" because he had been so skillful as a woodsman with the ax and maul. In the picture Abe, who once split a thousand rails for a pair of trousers, is cutting apart a stubborn split with his ax. The log falls apart and the loose splitting wedge drops out.

At their new place in Macon County, Illinois, Abe helped his father and family build a log cabin and make rails to fence in ten acres of land.

THE WINTER OF THE BIG SNOW . . .

FEBRUARY, 1831

By February, 1831, after snow storms had piled up snow two and three feet high that lay on the ground for two months, many of the pioneers who lived in lonely regions starved or froze to death, along with their livestock.

Short of food, the Lincolns needed help from their neighbors, so Abe set out on foot for William Warnick's cabin. While crossing a river he fell through the snow-covered ice, but trudged onward as his feet slowly became numb in the sub-zero weather. He made it to Warnick's, where Mrs. Warnick acted quickly. By rubbing "rabbit ile" grease on Abe's feet to take out the frostbite, she saved them.

After the hard winter, the Lincolns moved southeast in the spring.

52

DOWN THE SWOLLEN SANGAMON
BY CANOE . . . MARCH, 1831

In the spring of 1831 the county was so flooded that travel by land was not easy, so Lincoln, John Hanks, and John D. Johnston set out down the Sangamon River in a canoe. They were going to Springfield to see Denton Offutt, who wanted them to help him take a flatboat of produce down the Mississippi River to New Orleans.

Reconstructed replica of the original New Salem mill on the Sangamon River

Philip Van Doren Stern

53

ABE'S AUGER AND INGENUITY
SAVE THE DAY . . . 1831

Late in April, 1831, a crowd gathered on the river bank at the New Salem milldam to watch four men struggling with a stranded flatboat. The cargo-filled boat was stuck on the dam and could not be floated over it. The bow was raised in the air while water was coming into the stern, threatening to sink the boat. Tall Abe Lincoln sized up their situation and ordered the cargo in the stern unloaded. Denton Offutt, the owner, John Hanks, and John D. Johnston, the other boat-hands, worked until the water shifted to the bow and the boat righted itself. Then Abe went ashore, borrowed an auger, and bored a hole in the bow, letting the water run out. Then he plugged up the hole, and the lightened boat went easily over the dam, applauded by the onlookers. The flatboat was then taken on down the Mississippi River to New Orleans. When Lincoln returned to New Salem in August to make the village his home, many people remembered him because of the flatboat incident.

LINCOLN SEES A SLAVE MARKET . . .
MAY, 1831

At New Orleans, after a month's trip down the Mississippi by flatboat, Lincoln beheld the true horror of human slavery when he saw Negroes in chains. To his companions he said, "Slavery ran the iron into me then and there." Seeing the slave auction revolted him so much that he exclaimed to Denton Offutt, "Boy, let's get away from this. If ever I get a chance to hit that thing [slavery], I'll hit it hard."

IN HIS EARLY MANHOOD
LINCOLN MADE FRIENDS IN
NEW SALEM . . . 1831–1836

One of Abe Lincoln's many friends in the village was pretty Ann Rutledge, daughter of the keeper of Rutledge Tavern (*in background*), where Lincoln lived for a time. In New Salem, his adopted home for six years, Lincoln worked and studied, learned to be a surveyor, studied law, and was a captain in the militia. Besides, he was a storekeeper and postmaster, operated a gristmill and was a legislator.

Author's collection

New Salem scene

THE "SAMSON OF THE SANGAMON" . . . 1832

New Salem merchant Denton Offutt often bragged about the cleverness and strength of his clerk, Abraham Lincoln. The reckless and swaggering Clary's Grove boys quickly agreed that Abe was very clever, but they said that he would have to prove his strength. Their leader, Jack Armstrong, soon challenged Lincoln to a wrestling match. The town turned out and bets were placed, but neither man could throw the other. The match was a draw but Lincoln now "belonged," and the Armstrongs became Lincoln's fast friends.

57

LINCOLN PILOTS A RIVER STEAMBOAT . . . 1832

In the early spring of 1832 the steamboat *Talisman* came up the river routes from Cincinnati, loaded with a cargo of needed goods and merchandise. She came up the Sangamon from Beardstown while a crew of men, including Lincoln, cleared overhanging branches and snags from the stream. The *Talisman* puffed passed New Salem and docked at Bogue's mill as onlookers cheered. Many had never seen such a steamboat before.

Rowan Herndon of New Salem, an experienced boatman, was hired to pilot the *Talisman* back to Beardstown, and he chose Abe Lincoln to be his assistant. Each received forty dollars for piloting the steamboat back to Beardstown.

From the painting by George Catlin of Black Hawk, the Indian chief who led the Fox and Sauk tribes in the struggle to reclaim the corn lands he said were sold to the white men by Indians drunk with firewater. After Black Hawk crossed the Mississippi, the settlers got forces together to fight off his attacks.

A SUCCESS THAT GAVE
GREAT SATISFACTION . . . 1832

Young Lincoln worked at Offutt's store and mill until the Black Hawk War broke out. When he enlisted to fight in the war, his friends elected him captain of his company. Abe later exclaimed that he had "not since had any success in life which gave [him] so much satisfaction."

59

CAPTAIN LINCOLN
DEFENDS AN OLD INDIAN . . . 1832

One day an old Indian wandered into camp. He had a letter from
General Cass saying that he was friendly to whites. Some of the rough
soldiers believed that, "the only good Indian is a dead one," and since
they had enlisted to kill Indians, they felt he was a good one to start
with. But Captain Lincoln stepped in, backed up by most of the Clary's
Grove boys, and saved the old redskin's life.

ANCIENT OAKS FRAME THE PATH
LINCOLN WALKED IN NEW SALEM . . . 1832

While at New Salem, Lincoln studied from Kirkham's Grammar, and this copy shows samples of his handwriting. He gave the book to Ann Rutledge and wrote, "Ann M. Rutledge is now learning grammar."

Author's collection

Rowan Herndon's cabin near the trail leading to the mill, shown at dawn

SCENE IN NEW SALEM VILLAGE,
LINCOLN'S HOME FOR SIX YEARS . . . 1832

This photograph of New Salem in the spring shows the rustic cabins as they are now, after being rebuilt. The trough in the foreground is an ash hopper, used by the pioneers to make soap.

Below the photograph we see young Lincoln and Ann Rutledge studying together from a grammar book.

Josh Miller's New Salem
Blacksmith Shop

BLACKSTONE OR BLACKSMITH? . . . 1832

Hard-working blacksmith Joshua Miller made various pieces of iron-ware, such as hinges and door latches. Later he also shod horses and oxen for the people of New Salem.

Young Lincoln spent much time in Miller's shop, and at one time he seriously thought of taking up blacksmithing for a living. But when he acquired a copy of *Blackstone's Commentaries*, he found that the study of the law meant more to him. He told Josh of his newly found interest, knowing he had reached a turning point in his life.

"I'LL STUDY AND GET READY, AND
THEN THE CHANCE WILL COME . . ." 1834

In the quiet of the long and lonely winter nights, Lincoln studied late by the light of the fire. During his New Salem years he read Shakespeare, Burns, and books on grammar, surveying, and law, as well as any other books he could find to improve his education.

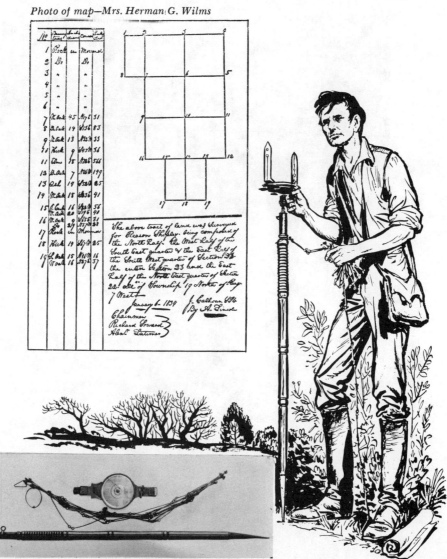

(*Above*) One of the first surveys made by Lincoln. Late in the year 1833 he became deputy surveyor to John Calhoun, the county surveyor; (*below*) Actual surveying instruments used by Lincoln, 1833–1835, preserved at the museum, New Salem

A. LINCOLN—DEPUTY SURVEYOR . . .

1833–1835

Lincoln bought a compass and chain on credit after mastering all his books on surveying in six weeks—studying day and night. His job paid three dollars a day, enabled him to pay his debts, buy bread, "and keep soul and body together."

New Salem scene

LINCOLN STUMPS FOR THE LEGISLATURE . . .

1832 AND 1834

At the urging of his friends, the tall, awkward young man decided to enter politics. In 1832 he talked to neighbors, farmers, and townspeople, hoping they would elect him to the legislature, but he lost—his only defeat by a direct vote of the people.

He tried again in 1834. This time he won. One man who saw him making a speech asked, "Can't the party raise any better material than that?" But after hearing Abe's speech the man was amazed that "he knew more than all the other candidates put together."

Major John T. Stuart, a lawyer, was also elected. He, more than anyone else, urged Lincoln to study law. He loaned Lincoln his law books so he could go "at it in good earnest."

66

Old state capitol at Vandalia

LINCOLN
THE LEGISLATOR...
1834

When Vandalia was the state capital of
Illinois in 1834, it was a town of about
one hundred buildings, mostly log
cabins, and had a population of about
six hundred. The old state capitol building still stands today (photograph). Lincoln took his seat as one of fifty-five
House members, having arrived by stagecoach December 1.

As a new member Lincoln played only
a minor part in the Legislature's work,
for which he received the welcome in-
come of three dollars a day, but because
he attended regularly, he missed few
roll calls. By observing the skilled poli-
ticians and lobbyists closely, he learned
much about his new life as a public
servant.

67

Author's collection

(*Above, right*) Sample of Lincoln's handwriting as postmaster . . . "P. M." is written after his signature of 1835; (*below, right*) a present-day New Salem postal stamp in use at the reconstructed New Salem log building U. S. Post Office (*above, left*), at New Salem State Park, Ill.

POSTMASTER LINCOLN . . . 1833 TO 1836

Lincoln served as postmaster in New Salem, Illinois, from May 7, 1833, to May 30, 1836. As postmaster he sent and received mail without paying the postal rates, and he marked his letters, "Free, A. Lincoln," with the date. He did quite satisfactory work during his time as postmaster, often walking several miles to deliver a letter he thought important, although at times he was careless about leaving his office open and unlocked during the day. And of course he enjoyed reading all the newspapers that came in.

68

Part of a page from the Sangamo *Journal* of March 26, 1836, showing Lincoln's advertisement for his lost horse and an advertisement for a sale of lots in Huron, a town he once surveyed

LINCOLN VALUED THE NEWSPAPERS . . .
MARCH 26, 1836

As we know, from his earliest years Abe Lincoln read every book or newspaper he could find. He knew how much they had taught him, and soon he realized how much newspapers formed public opinion. Later in his political career, on May 30, 1859, he even secretly bought, for $400, a small newspaper printed in German and English, the weekly Illinois *Staats-Anzeiger*.

69

LINCOLN—YOUNG LAWYER . . .

1836–1837

The long and lonely hours Lincoln spent studying law books finally paid off. In the fall of 1836 he was given a law license, and by March 1, 1837, his name was entered on the roll of attorneys in the Supreme Court Clerk's office. Here we see Abe being sworn in.

On April 12, 1837, the Springfield paper announced: "J. T. Stuart and A. Lincoln, Attorneys and Counsellors at Law, will practice conjointly in the courts of this Judicial Circuit. Office No. 4, Hoffman's Row, upstairs."

At that time Stuart was running for Congress, so his new young partner had to handle almost all the law practice alone. Thus Lincoln learned law the hard way, through practical experience.

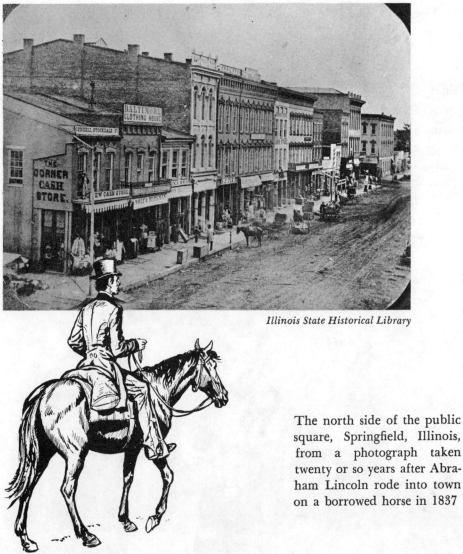

Illinois State Historical Library

The north side of the public square, Springfield, Illinois, from a photograph taken twenty or so years after Abraham Lincoln rode into town on a borrowed horse in 1837

LINCOLN MOVES TO SPRINGFIELD . . . 1837

Right after he arrived in Springfield, Lincoln went to the general store where he met Joshua Speed, a clerk, and asked for credit, telling Speed he could not then pay for a single night's lodging. But if and when his "experiment as a lawyer" was a success, he would pay. Speed offered to share his lodgings upstairs with the melancholy newcomer, and the two soon became lifelong friends.

71

LINCOLN BOWS, MARY CURTSIES . . .
1839

When, in 1839, the attractive twenty-one-year-old Mary Todd came from Lexington, Kentucky, to visit with her sister, Mrs. Ninian Edwards, she found she had many admirers, among them Stephen A. Douglas and Abraham Lincoln.

At a social affair one evening Abe asked, "Miss Todd, I should like to dance with you the worst way," adding that he had never danced much except "behind a plow." Mary accepted, and later agreed he did dance in the "very worst way."

(*Author's collection*)

Farmington Museum,
Louisville, Ky.

BEAUTIFUL, RESTFUL FARMINGTON . . . 1841

Once, when Lincoln had a bad case of the blues and was near a nervous breakdown, a change of scenery was prescribed. His good friend, Joshua Speed, invited him to visit the Speed family home near Louisville. So, from the middle of August to September 7, Lincoln enjoyed the hospitality of the Speed family and returned to Springfield a happier and much improved man.

73

ABRAHAM LINCOLN AND MARY TODD
ARE MARRIED . . . NOVEMBER 4, 1842

On November 4, 1842, with a few close friends and members of the family present, Mary Todd and Abraham Lincoln were married by the Reverend Charles Dresser, at the home of Mary's sister and brother-in-law, Mr. and Mrs. Ninian W. Edwards. Engraved inside the wedding ring Abe placed on Mary's finger were the words "Love is eternal."

Long after the quiet evening ceremony, Mary's sister, Frances Todd Wallace, who was there, declared, "And they certainly did live happily together—as much so as any man and woman I have ever known."

Chicago Historical Society

THE NEWLYWEDS FIND A HOME—
THE GLOBE TAVERN . . . 1842

Hand in hand, Abraham and Mary Lincoln set out to find a home in Springfield. For about a year and a half the newlyweds lived at the Globe Tavern. Here their first son, Robert Todd Lincoln, was born on August 1, 1843. By spring of the next year they were able to buy a cottage of their own—from the man who had married them two years before, the Reverend Charles Dresser.

(*Bottom, left, and right*) Abraham and Mary Lincoln a few years after they had purchased their little home, when Abraham was 37 and Mary was 28 years of age.

Taken from daguerreotypes by N. H. Shepherd in 1846, these two portraits were on view in the Lincoln home as long as their son Robert could remember. They are now in the Library of Congress.

THE LINCOLNS BUY A HOME . . .

MAY 2, 1844

The only home the Lincolns ever owned was located at Eighth and Jackson streets in Springfield. The sketch shows the house as it appeared in 1844 when Lincoln bought it from Reverend Dresser. It cost $1,500. Abe and Mary's first child, Robert Todd, was not yet a year old.

Later, in April, 1856, they had the house remodeled to a full two stories. It was their home for seventeen years, until they moved to the White House.

76

Photograph of S. F. B. Morse painting—Corcoran Gallery of Art.

CONGRESSMAN LINCOLN . . . 1847–1848

In 1846, after eight years in the Illinois Legislature, Lincoln was elected to a term in the Congress of the United States. Here he appears dressed in the costume of the day as a thirty-nine-year-old Representative making a speech to his fellow Congressmen.

77

This 1848 daguerreotype shows the typical river steamers like those the Lincolns used when they traveled.

MR. LINCOLN GOES TO CONGRESS . . . 1847

The Lincolns, Abe carrying four-year-old Bobby and Mary carrying the baby, Eddie, traveled east by stagecoach, steamboat, and railroad in the cool October and November weather.

But before reaching Washington, D.C., they stopped at St. Louis, Missouri, Frankfort, Kentucky, and finally Lexington, to visit friends and relatives. Mary Lincoln's brothers and sisters enjoyed seeing her for the first time since her marriage.

By the second of December they had arrived in Washington, taking lodgings at Brown's Hotel.

LINCOLN THE INVENTOR . . . 1849

Abraham Lincoln had had a lot of experience in shallow-water river boating. In 1849 he invented a method that enabled river boats to lift themselves off shoals and sand bars. He built an eighteen-inch model with a system of pulleys, pumps, and water chambers that would empty if the craft got stuck, making the boat lighter. Lincoln was granted Patent No. 6469, becoming the only President who ever received a patent. Today the principle of his invention is used on submarines.

Smithsonian Institution

Lincoln Patent Model

79

Preston Butler's 1859 camera view of the east side of the public square in Springfield. The Corneau and Diller store is near the center of the picture.

LINCOLN, A FAMILIAR FIGURE
ON SPRINGFIELD STREETS . . . 1850'S

The tall, black-clad figure of lawyer Lincoln, chatting with his friends, was a well-known sight to the townspeople of Springfield. Here we see Mr. Lincoln talking over the day's news with companions as they pause in front of Corneau and Diller's drugstore.

LINCOLN JOKES
WHILE HE MAKES
HIS PURCHASE . . .
1850'S

The business ledgers from Lincoln's favorite drugstore, Corneau and Diller's, still exist today, showing various entries to Lincoln's account.

Here we see Lincoln joking as he examines the bottle of medicine he has just bought and as druggist Roland Weaver Diller makes the entry in the ledger.

CORNEAU'S DRUG STORE, ABE'S
FAVORITE CONVERSATION PLACE . . . 1850'S

Lincoln's favorite place for loafing and chatting with close friends was around the back stove at Corneau and Diller's drugstore. Lincoln liked to swap stories and opinions with old friends. The scene above was typical of the year 1850: Lincoln gestures to his rival in later years, Stephen A. Douglas. His former law partner, Stephen T. Logan, listens as he whittles on a stick—and sometimes on the arm of a drugstore chair. Good friend Judge David Davis is amused at Lincoln's story.

81

RIDING THE CIRCUIT . . . 1850'S

Each spring and fall, lawyer Lincoln set out on his law-practice tour of the courts of his judicial circuit, a life he loved well. Most often he traveled in his open buggy, behind his own horse. And when alone he often read as he rode along.

Taken about 1852, this is a daguerreotype, never published before, of Lincoln's freckled-faced friend, George P. Davis.

THE LAD WHO RODE WITH LINCOLN ... 1850'S

George Perrin Davis, the ten-year-old son of Lincoln's good friend Judge David Davis, rode the circuit once in Abraham's buggy. Lawyer Lincoln told his young friend all about his horse, Old Buck. George remembered their travels together for a long time, and often asked about Old Buck.

Lincoln's home, Eighth and Jackson streets, Springfield, Ill. (*Left*) photograph by Whipple, 1860; (*right*) photo by author a century later, 1961

LINCOLN, INDULGENT FATHER . . . 1856

Mr. and Mrs. Lincoln had four sons. Robert, born in 1843, was the oldest. Eddie, born in 1846, lived only four years. Willie was born in 1850, the year Eddie died. Thomas, better known as Tad, was born in 1853.

Neighbors said that at times they saw Lincoln in his shirt sleeves, walking up and down in front of his house, pulling the two youngest boys in a little wagon. Often he was deep in thought, not noticing his surroundings or whether or not his youngsters were enjoying their ride.

Photograph of the original name plate at the
Illinois State Historical Library, Springfield

MR. LINCOLN GETS "HELP"

FROM HIS BOYS . . . 1858

Putting a new name plate on the front door of his home was a task
Lincoln shared with little Willie and Tad. "A. Lincoln" became a
nationally known name later in 1858, after the famous debates with
Stephen A. Douglas.

85

DUFF ARMSTRONG'S
MURDER TRIAL ...
1857–1858

William D. "Duff"
Armstrong as a sol-
dier in 1861

*Lincoln Museum,
New Salem, Ill.*

In May, 1858, Hannah Armstrong, the widow of Jack Armstrong, asked Mr. Lincoln to help her son, Duff, who was going on trial for the murder of Preston Metzker on the night of August 29, 1857. Because of his long friendship with Jack and Hannah, Lincoln was glad to offer his services and defend Duff without asking for a fee.

A witness for the prosecution said he had seen Duff commit murder at half past nine by the light of a bright moon.

Lincoln then produced the almanac for August, 1857, which showed that the moon, slightly past its first quarter, had given practically no light that night.

THE 1857 ALMANAC, AND THE PAGE
FOR AUGUST ... 1857–1858

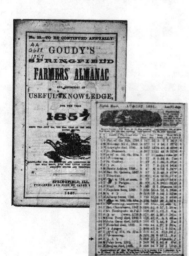

Lincoln's dramatic presentation of the 1857 Almanac, showing the position of the moon, was very important in clearing Duff of the murder charge. It helped to prove the witness's story to be false.

Cover page and the month of August page for the 1857 Almanac, possibly the edition Lincoln used at the trial

Illinois State Historical Library

James T. Hickey

The Hall of Representatives where Lincoln made his forceful speech, photographed at a later date

THE "HOUSE DIVIDED" SPEECH . . .

JUNE 16, 1858

At the State Republican Convention, which met in the Illinois House of Representatives, it was agreed by everyone "that Abraham Lincoln is the first and only choice of the Republicans of Illinois for the U.S. Senate." That night Lincoln delivered his House Divided Speech, in which he said, "A house divided against itself cannot stand. I believe this government cannot endure permanently half slave and half free. . . . It will become all one thing, or all the other." His words were like dynamite; they brought him to the attention of the entire nation and paved the way for the famous Lincoln-Douglas debates in the fall.

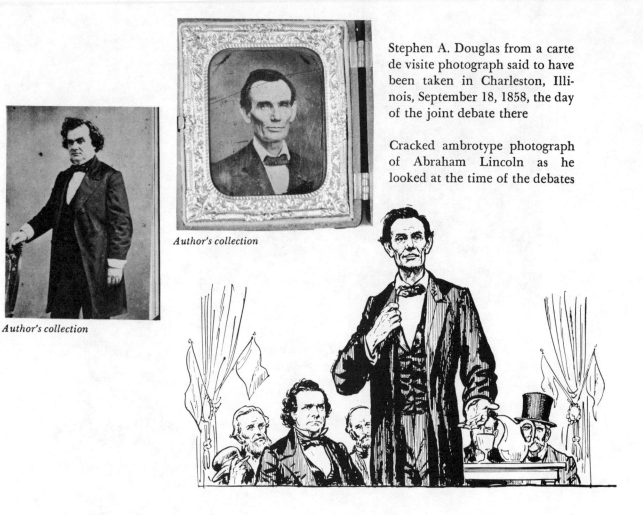

Stephen A. Douglas from a carte de visite photograph said to have been taken in Charleston, Illinois, September 18, 1858, the day of the joint debate there

Cracked ambrotype photograph of Abraham Lincoln as he looked at the time of the debates

Author's collection

Author's collection

THE LINCOLN—DOUGLAS DEBATES . . . 1858

The most famous debates in American history were sparked by the Senate race in Illinois between Abraham Lincoln and Stephen A. Douglas. Both went up and down the state making speeches, and they appeared together in seven joint debates.

Douglas traveled in grand style, in his own special railroad car, with a brass band and a cannon to salute his arrivals. Lincoln detested much of the "fizzlegigs and fireworks" offered him by enthusiastic reception committees. He liked to arrive in town quietly, sometimes on a humble hayrig. At other times he rode on freight trains—his party's way of showing contempt for Douglas's elegance.

Lincoln lost the Senate race, but gained national recognition. He comforted himself by saying, "I am after larger game; the battle of 1860 is worth a hundred of this."

HIS HONOR, "JUDGE" LINCOLN . . . 1859

During Lincoln's years as a lawyer, it was common practice for circuit judges, when taking a rest from their duties, to have attorneys sit on the bench in their place.

Often Judge David Davis called on Lincoln to take the bench when he was away.

"Judge" Lincoln presided in thirty-four cases of the Logan County Court from March 21 to April 2, 1859. He was highly respected by his fellow lawyers for his wisdom and fair judgment.

LINCOLN'S FARTHEST VISIT WEST . . . AUGUST 12, 1859

In 1859, with his friend Ozias M. Hatch of Springfield, Lincoln took a business and pleasure trip to examine land at Council Bluffs, Iowa. The two men traveled by railway to Quincy, Illinois, crossed the river to St. Joseph, Missouri, and took the steamer *Campbell* for Council Bluffs. On August 12 they arrived and took a sight-seeing trip with friends. From Cemetery Hill, north of town, they viewed the vast countryside that lay to the north, south, and west. This was the farthest west that Lincoln traveled in the United States.

89

POLITICAL CAMPAIGNER . . . 1859

The political speeches Lincoln made in the fall of 1859 reviewed the arguments he had made during the previous year, in the Lincoln-Douglas debates of 1858. The picture of him talking in Dayton, Ohio, in front of the courthouse, is a typical scene of his speech-making tour.

A photograph of the lost painting made September 17 and 18, 1859, by Charles Nickum

Author's collection

LINCOLN AND THE YOUNG ARTIST . . .

SEPTEMBER, 1859

As Lincoln's fame grew he was asked more and more to pose for photographers. Once while he sat for his picture in Cridland's Gallery in Dayton, a fifteen-year-old boy, Charles Nickum, made a sketch of him. As the boy painted, Lincoln said smilingly, "Keep on; you may make a good one, but never a pretty one."

LINCOLN POSES FOR BRADY

IN NEW YORK, FEBRUARY 27, 1860

In 1860 the tall lawyer from Illinois posed for Mathew B. Brady for the first time. Lincoln himself was said to have made the remark that the Cooper Union speech and this Brady photograph made him President.

Author's collection

One of the actual carte de visite photographs made by the Brady gallery from the life negative the famous photographer made in 1860, at the time of Lincoln's Cooper Union speech

THE COOPER UNION SPEECH...

FEBRUARY 27, 1860

Three months before Lincoln was nominated for the Presidency, he was little known in New York. But what he said on the evening he spoke to 1,500 people at the Cooper Institute helped to make him President. In the basement of the Cooper Union building, some of New York's most important people assembled to hear the speech, including editors William Cullen Bryant, Horace Greeley, Theodore Tilton, and Henry J. Raymond.

An observer described the tall, gangling speaker as wearing a new black suit that was creased from being packed in his valise; "his bushy head, with stiff black hair thrown back . . . balanced on a lean headstalk. . . ." Lincoln started the speech poorly, but later he held the audience's respectful attention for almost an hour and a half. Besides the gentle hiss of the gaslights, the only thing that could be heard was Lincoln's voice as he concluded: "Let us have faith that right makes might, and in that faith, let us to the end dare to do our duty as we understand it."

(*Above*) This early photograph shows Volk at work in his studio; (*below*) this old photograph shows a profile of the original cast of a life mask of Lincoln's face, made on March 31, 1860. The sculptor used the mask to aid him in making the plaster bust.

LINCOLN SITS FOR A CHICAGO SCULPTOR . . . 1860

Toward the end of March, 1860, during his free time between court sessions in Chicago, Lincoln gave sittings to sculptor Leonard Wells Volk, who made a bust of him.

94

Author's collection

Stake-and-rider, zig-zag rail fence,
New Salem, like those split by Lincoln
and John Hanks

THE "RAIL-SPLITTER" CANDIDATE . . . 1860

Before the 1860 Illinois State Republican Convention at Decatur, Lincoln's friend Richard Oglesby was talking to John Hanks and learned about the rail fence Lincoln and Hanks had built back in 1830, west of Decatur. Oglesby got the idea of taking Hanks out to the old Lincoln farm and find some of the rails. He had John carry a couple of them into the convention hall with a banner that read:

ABRAHAM LINCOLN THE RAIL CANDIDATE FOR PRESIDENT IN 1860
TWO RAILS FROM A LOT OF 3000 MADE IN 1830 BY JOHN HANKS AND
ABE LINCOLN, WHOSE FATHER WAS THE FIRST PIONEER IN
MACON COUNTY.

So it was that the "Rail-splitter Candidate" was born, soon to capture the public's imagination.

95

Old ambrotype of Abraham Lincoln (mounted reversed) from one of four campaign photographs taken early in June by Alexander Hesler

Author's collection

Author's collection

The Wigwam, Chicago, 1860, where Lincoln was nominated by the Republican Party for the Presidency of the United States

LINCOLN IS NOMINATED . . . MAY 18, 1860

At home in Springfield, Lincoln received the news wired from Chicago. At the Illinois *State Journal* office, editor Edward L. Baker handed Lincoln the dispatch. An eyewitness said that Lincoln's features at first showed great joy and then a look of serious responsibility. Friends there gave him rousing cheers and rushed to shake his hand. Abe said, "There is a lady over on Eighth Street who is deeply interested in this news. I will carry it to her." And off he strode.

He was stopped by a boy from the telegraph office, carrying the message he already knew. Thanking the lad for the note, he continued on to his house and "Molly," carrying the paper in his hand.

96

LINCOLN RECEIVES THE NOMINATION AND
THE PARTY LEADERS AT HOME . . .

MAY 19, 1860

A delegation of important Republicans journeyed from the Chicago Convention to Springfield to give Lincoln formal notice of his nomination for the Presidency. Lincoln received the gentlemen warmly, and before they left many felt that the party's choice was no ordinary man.

L. M. U. collection

(*Left*) The next month, newspapers and campaign printed matter displayed Lincoln's portrait as best they could.

(*Right*) The first time Lincoln ever had his picture in the paper was June 30, 1860, in the Vincennes *Weekly Gazette*. The newspaper hired an artist at great expense to make a woodcut engraving from a photograph.

O. V. Brown

97

Mrs. Arthur S. Wright

This 1860 campaign portrait was pasted in a scrapbook at the time by Illinois Wide-Awaker N. S. Wright.

"WIDE AWAKES" FOR LINCOLN . . . 1860

All over the country Wide Awake Clubs were started, and they marched in torchlight processions night after night for Lincoln and Hamlin, the Republican candidate for Vice-President. They dressed in oilcloth uniforms and caps and carried banners, torches, or lanterns through crowded streets, singing the praises of "Honest Abe." Eight campaign biographies were printed; medals, badges, buttons, and leaflets were handed out. Paintings and photographs of Lincoln were displayed, announcing the party's choice.

Photos—Preston Butler

LINCOLN SITS FOR A HOME-TOWN

PHOTOGRAPHER . . . AUGUST 13, 1860

This 1859 photograph of the south side of the public square, Springfield, was the work of Preston Butler and shows (*arrow*) his gallery building. Lincoln visited here several times, and the oval portrait (*inset*) was made there in 1860. The drawing shows photographer Butler in action, getting Lincoln's likeness.

Early in 1960, one hundred years after Lincoln's visits, the old gallery building was torn down. The photographer's west wall and top-floor skylight were still intact at the time.

A LITTLE GIRL WRITES A REQUEST . . . 1860

NY
WESTFIELD CHATAUQUE CO
Oct 15. 1860

HON A B LINCOLN
DEAR SIR

My father has just home from the fair and brought home your picture and Mr. Hamlin's. I am a little girl only eleven years old, but want you should be President of the United States very much so I hope you wont think me very bold to write to such a great man as you are. Have you any little girls about as large as I am if so give them my love and tell her to write to me if you cannot answer this letter. I have got 4 brother's and part of them will vote for you any way and if you will let your whiskers grow I will try and get the rest of them to vote for you you would look a great deal better for your face is so thin. All the ladies like whiskers and they would tease their husband's to vote for you and then you would be President. My father is going to vote for you and if I was a man I would vote for you to but I will try and get every one to vote for you that I can I think that rail fence around your picture makes it look very pretty I have got a little baby sister she is nine weeks old and is just as cunning as can be. When you direct your letter dir[e]ct to Grace Bedell Westfield Chatauque County New York

I must not write any more answer this letter right off Good bye

GRACE BEDELL

Author's collection

H. D. Billings, Delphos, Kansas

(*Top left*) Grace Bedell; (*bottom left*) Lincoln *before* he grew his beard; (*top right*) Grace Bedell's letter and envelope. The author's conception of twelve-year-old Grace Bedell, who wrote a letter to Lincoln in 1860, suggesting that he grow a beard. (Likeness adapted from an early photograph of Miss Bedell as a young lady, and painted in the style of the old photographic poses of the day.)

100

H. D. Billings, Delphos, Kansas

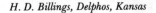

(*Top left*) President-elect Lincoln, February 9, 1861, *after* he had grown his famous beard; (*bottom*) Lincoln's letter to Grace Bedell

President-elect Lincoln stopped at Westfield, N. Y. on his way to Washington. Greeting little Grace with a kiss, he said, "You see, Grace, I let these whiskers grow just for you. How do you like the improvement you advised me to make?"

LINCOLN DECIDES TO GROW A BEARD . . . 1861

Private

SPRINGFIELD, ILLS. Oct. 19. 1860

MISS GRACE BEDELL
MY DEAR LITTLE MISS.

Your very agreeable letter of the 15th. is received.

I regret the necessity of saying I have no daughters. I have three sons— one seventeen, one nine, and one seven, years of age. They, with their mother, constitute my whole family.

As to the whiskers, having never worn any, do you not think people would call it a piece of silly affection if I were to begin it now? Your very sincere well-wisher

A. Lincoln.

101

LINCOLN HELPS A LITTLE GIRL IN DISTRESS . . . 1861

A never-to-be-forgotten kindness by Lincoln turned tears into joy for a little neighborhood girl who stood crying at her gate one day. She had planned for a long time to visit a little friend, and she was unhappy because the hackman had failed to pick up her trunk and take it to the railroad station. Now she would miss her train, she thought. Abraham Lincoln happened along and asked why she was crying. When she told him he said, "Oh, ho, wipe your eyes and come quick!" Lincoln got the heavy trunk, shouldered it, and strode down the street, while the little girl trotted behind, drying her tears. They reached the station in time! Mr. Lincoln kissed his little neighbor good-by and told her to have a good time.

GOOD-BY TO LAW OFFICE AND PARTNER . . . 1861

Shortly before leaving for Washington, President-elect Lincoln made his last visit to his law office, put his papers in order, and told his junior partner, William H. Herndon: "The election of a President makes no change in the firm of Lincoln and Herndon; for if I live I'm coming back . . . and we'll resume practice . . . let the office sign remain."

The old photograph shows the west side of Springfield's public square. The next to the last building in the block (*arrow*) was the location of the Lincoln and Herndon law office for many years.

Author's collection

Log cabin on Goosenest Prairie
in 1891

LINCOLN BIDS FAREWELL
TO HIS STEPMOTHER . . . 1861

Before President-elect Lincoln went to Washington he paid a last visit
to his stepmother in Coles County. He went to the log cabin on Goosenest Prairie which he had helped his father build when he was twenty-
one years old. Arriving on the morning of January 31, 1861, he found
that the cabin chimney had fallen down, and his second cousin, John
Hall, was repairing it. Hall told Mr. Lincoln where to find his stepmother; she had left the day before to stay with some relatives at Farmington, Illinois. But first Lincoln wanted to see his father's grave. He
took two pieces of wood, and carving the letters *T. L.* in the stakes,
drove them into the ground at the head and foot of the grave.

Later, at Farmington, Abraham warmly greeted his stepmother and
gave her the present of a black woolen dress. After a pleasant dinner
and visit with his folks he bade her his last farewell.

FAREWELL TO HIS SPRINGFIELD FRIENDS . . .
FEBRUARY 11, 1861

Departing from his home in Springfield, Illinois, for the White House, President-elect Lincoln bade his friends and neighbors a touching and prophetic good-by. He never returned again in life.

MY FRIENDS: No one, not in my situation, can appreciate my feeling of sadness at this parting. To this place, and the kindness of these people, I owe everything. Here I have lived a quarter of a century, and have passed from a young to an old man. Here my children have been born, and one is buried. I now leave, not knowing when, or whether ever, I may return, with a task before me greater than that which rested upon Washington. Without the assistance of that Divine Being, who ever attended him, I cannot succeed. With that assistance I cannot fail. Trusting in Him, who can go with me, and remain with you, and be everywhere for good, let us confidently hope that all will yet be well. To His care commending you, as I hope in your prayers you will commend me, I bid you an affectionate farewell.

OHIO IS HOST TO LINCOLN ON HIS

FIFTY-SECOND BIRTHDAY . . . FEBRUARY 12, 1861

President-elect Lincoln was on his way to greatness in February of 1861 as his inaugural train headed for Washington. At various stops and cities on his twelve-day train ride he was enthusiastically greeted by thousands of well-wishers. The way the Cincinnati citizens greeted him on his fifty-second birthday, on February 12, 1861, was typical of how he was received all along the way. The people believed that Honest Abe would do his very best in the great task that lay before him.

THE LITTLE BOY'S GREETING . . .
FEBRUARY 18, 1861

As the President-elect's train made ready to roll out of the decorated Rochester, New York station, a small boy climbed up the back platform of the train.

Cheerily he said, "How do you do, Mr. Lincoln!"

The tall man reached down and shook the little fellow's hand. Then, in a thoughtful and fatherly manner, he cautioned the boy to be careful when he got off, so he would not get hurt.

A SECRET RAILROAD RIDE AT NIGHT
FOR THE PRESIDENT-ELECT . . . 1861

There was a rumor of a plot in 1861 to assassinate Abraham Lincoln at Baltimore, Maryland, before his train reached Washington for his inauguration. Friends persuaded Lincoln to cancel his plans to visit Baltimore and go ahead of schedule to the capital.

A story was circulated that Lincoln wore a disguise—a Scotch cap and a long military cloak—as he secretly left the Harrisburg station on the evening of February 22. What he actually did was to discard his familiar tall hat and wear an old overcoat he had brought along with him from Springfield. He was able to slip out of town unnoticed, with his trusted friend and bodyguard Ward Hill Lamon and detective Allan Pinkerton, who had discovered the plot.

CROWDS ASSEMBLE FOR LINCOLN'S
FIRST INAUGURAL . . . 1861

On March 4, 1861 the people gathered in front of the still-unfinished Capitol to see the inaugural ceremonies. Soldiers had been stationed around the building in case of emergency. The President-elect read his address calmly, and after bowing a response to the applause, took the official oath of office.

Lincoln's first inauguration

LINCOLN'S
FIRST INAUGURAL MESSAGE
TRAVELS FROM COAST TO COAST . . . 1861

The famous pony express had begun its fast overland mail delivery eleven months before, on April 3, 1860, from St. Joseph, Missouri, to Sacramento, California.

The record for that run was made in March, 1861, when Lincoln's inaugural address was carried over the route in seven days and eleven hours. It usually took the fleet-footed ponies eight to ten days to cover that distance.

110

A PHOTO FOR A KISS . . . 1861

White House neighbor Julia Taft was in the sitting room with Mrs. Lincoln one day when the President came in with a lot of Brady photographs. He said, "Julie, do you want my picture?"

"Oh, yes, sir . . ."

"Give me a kiss, then you can have it."

She kissed him on the cheek, and Mr. Lincoln said, "Now we'll pick out a good one." The one they chose is copied above.

Author's collection

The picture of the President Julie picked.

WAR! FORT SUMTER BOMBARDED . . .

APRIL 12 AND 13, 1861

The first shot was fired on April 12, 1861, and the Civil War between the North and South began. People watched from the housetops in Charleston as the battle raged around Fort Sumter. Major Robert Anderson's Union troops, inside the fort, held out against General Beauregard's pounding for thirty-three hours. Without enough food, they finally had to give up. As Anderson and his men boarded a relief ship headed north for New York, they saw the new Confederate flag, the Stars and Bars, flying above the fort they had surrendered.

112

THE COMMANDER-IN-CHIEF REVIEWS
HIS TROOPS . . . 1861

The city of Washington was practically turned into a vast military camp as troops moved in and set up their arms and equipment. Almost daily President Lincoln visited the forts and camps in and around the capital city, and the Commander-in-Chief saw many troop parades and reviews. The soldier boys called him Father Abraham; they often wrote home about his frequent visits among them, and commented on how well he rode and handled his horse.

This is a rare photograph of Colonel E. E. Ellsworth, Lincoln's young protegé, a strange and fascinating adventurer.

DEATH OF A YOUNG COLONEL . . . MAY 24, 1861

Dashing young Colonel Elmer Ephraim Ellsworth had been a law student in Lincoln and Herndon's law office, and, a born soldier, had organized a crack Zouave drill troop that caught the country's fancy. Lincoln became very fond of him.

He had made campaign speeches in 1860, and it appeared that his fame and national popularity were second only to Lincoln's.

On May 24, 1861, his blossoming career was cut short; he became the first commissioned officer to lose his life in the Civil War. He died as he had lived, madly in love with action. When he tore the Confederate flag from the roof of the Marshall House in Alexandria, Virginia, hotel proprietor James W. Jackson shot him. Ellsworth's corporal, Francis E. Brownell, in turn shot Jackson. The Lincolns grieved at Ellsworth's death, and held funeral services for him in the East Room of the White House on May 25, 1861.

114

THE DEFEATED—AFTER BULL RUN . . . JULY 21, 1861

The wounded and exhausted Northern troops streamed into Washington soon after their defeat in the Battle of Bull Run. General McDowell's withdrawal turned into a rout, and his disorganized troops could scarcely be stopped short of Washington, twenty-five miles away, as the battle raged. With this first defeat, the North fully realized they now had a real war on their hands with the Southern Confederacy.

LINCOLN PARDONS A SLEEPING
SENTINEL . . . SEPTEMBER, 1861

Eighteen-year-old William Scott of Company K, Third Vermont, volunteered to take guard duty for a sick comrade, and passed the night as a sentinel. The very next night he himself was detailed for the same guard duty. He was so tired that he fell asleep at his post. He was then tried and sentenced to die in twenty-four hours. A committee of his comrades tried in vain to save his life, and finally, in desperation, went to see President Lincoln.

Lincoln visited the camp prison and called on the sad-faced boy, to hear his story. The lad's only request was that the men who had to shoot him be from another regiment. Lincoln said, "My boy, you are not going to be shot tomorrow. I believe you when you tell me you could not stay awake. I am going to send you back to your regiment." The thankful boy promised to do his duty to repay the President's great kindness.

LINCOLN WITH HIS FRIENDS . . . 1861

Lincoln was known as the story-telling President. During the dark days of the Civil War, the Chief Executive would often tell funny stories to his friends—sometimes to illustrate a point and sometimes to defend himself against unreasonable requests, but most of all to relieve his mind from the awful strain of the war. Once, when criticized for telling jokes, the President said, "Were it not for this occasional vent, I would die. I must laugh to keep from crying."

His friends noticed that when he got to the point, or "nub," as he called it, of the story, his face would light up and his eyes sparkle with fun, and he would laugh as heartily as anyone.

LINCOLN'S BOYS
IN THE WHITE HOUSE . . .
1861–1862

(*Above, left*) Tad Lincoln's miniature brass cannon, a model of Capt. Dahlgren's boat howitzer, is now preserved in the Illinois State Historical Library along with the President's note:

> Oct. 14, 1862
> *Capt. Dahlgren may let "Tad" have a little gun that he cannot hurt himself with.*

This toy gun was the result of Tad's visit with his father to the Navy Yard, where he saw the miniatures; (*center, left*) Tad and Willie Lincoln had many pets at the White House, including rabbits, goats, and ponies. The photograph shows Tad on his pony; (*below, left*) Thomas "Tad" Lincoln, pictured here dressed in one of his soldier suits, a lieutenant with small dress sword. Tad was dashing, brave and often impudent; (*below, right*) William Wallace Lincoln posed in 1861 like the little gentleman he was. Willie was most like his father—thoughtful, studious, and imaginative; he enjoyed books and was a grave, delicate boy.

Library of Congress

National Archives

Chicago Historical Society

118

A PLAY IN THE ATTIC . . . 1861–1862

The spacious attic of the White House contained the castoff belongings of former occupants, and was the Lincoln boys' favorite place to play. Once they gave a play there; Tad called it a circus. Willie printed the programs, and everybody in the White House staff was invited—anyone with five cents admission. Even the President came. Tad dressed in his mother's clothes and wore his father's spectacles. Willie played the banjo and sang songs. The President enjoyed their antics so much that "he laughed all over."

AN ASSIST FROM FATHER ABRAHAM . . . 1861–1862

Despite the heavy burdens of his office, President Lincoln spent much time with his youngest sons, Willie and Tad. He could often be seen walking down the street or through the White House halls with one of his boys riding on his shoulders.

Lincoln is pictured here as he may have looked on a cold day in the winter of 1861–1862 when he stopped to help his sons build a snow fort in front of the White House.

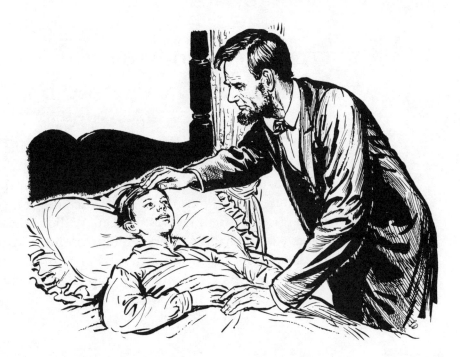

LOOKING IN ON HIS AILING SON . . . 1862

President Lincoln always took time out to give fatherly concern to his boys in their troubles and illnesses.

In February, 1862, both Willie, eleven, and Tad, eight, were seriously sick in bed. Sadly, Willie passed away. Now the President, like many fathers in the land, had lost a son during the terrible war.

Fortunately, Tad recovered, and during another illness later in March, father Abraham encouraged him with the gift of a check (*above*), which he could cash at the bank "when well enough to present."

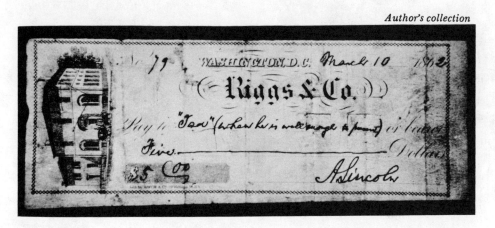

BATTLE OF THE MONITOR AND
THE MERRIMAC . . . MARCH 8 AND 9, 1862

A worried President and confident Secretary of the Navy, Gideon Welles, looked out of the White House office window while they awaited news of the battle between the ironclad warships. War Secretary Stanton was frantic and wild with rage because the Confederate ironclad *Merrimac* was approaching Washington. Welles remained calm, sure that his navy would handle things with the *Monitor*. After six hours the battle at Hampton Roads was a draw, but it proved that the days of wooden warships was at an end. The capital had been defended, and the North was safe from naval attack.

Author's collection

(*Inset*) Currier and Ives print showing the *Monitor* (called the "cheesebox on a raft") with her two-gun turret meeting the Confederate ironclad *Merrimac,* which had ten guns

Facing President Lincoln, General George B. McClellan poses with members of his staff for photographer Alexander Gardner, Mathew Brady's top cameraman.

LINCOLN VISITS GENERAL McCLELLAN . . .

OCTOBER 1 TO 4, 1862

Just two weeks after the Emancipation Proclamation (September 22, 1862), the worried President conferred with "Little Mac," General McClellan, and urged him to take the offensive to crush the rebellion. What seemed to be inaction on McClellan's part often caused Lincoln to say, "He's got the slows."

123

THE CIVIL WAR—AT FIRST,
CAMP LIFE AND PARADES . . . 1861

Author's collection

Author's collection

Union Bluebelly

Leisure time in camp recorded by an unknown tintype artist. This photo by Mathew B. Brady of a cavalry officer and his mount shows the spit and polish typical of the early days of the Civil War.

LATER, THE CRUEL ADVENTURE IN
FIGHTING, DESTRUCTION, AND DEATH . . . 1865

This little-known photograph of Richmond in ruins, 1865, reflects the war's desolation.

Photo—L. M. U. collection, unpublished

Photo—L. M. U. collection, unpublished

Johnny Reb, from the First
Virginia Cavalry

The Union army's medical men pose for a picture that reveals the care given to the wounded, a scene familiar to both sides in the war.

125

TAD LINCOLN'S GOATS . . . 1861–1863

The Lincoln boys were fond of pets, and one of Tad's favorites was his nanny goat.

One day a party of Boston ladies were admiring the velvet carpet and plush-upholstered furniture in the East Room. Suddenly a shrill voice rang out: "Look out there!" and young Tad came through with a pair of goats hitched to a kitchen chair. He was driving them with a long whip.

Tad's nanny goat finally disappeared one day while Tad was away on vacation with his mother. His father wrote that Nanny was last seen "resting herself and chewing her little cud on the middle of Tad's bed; but now she's gone!"

SOLDIER'S MASCOT NAMED FOR
LINCOLN . . . 1863

During the Civil War the Union soldiers called President Lincoln "Father Abraham" and "Old Abe." The most famous mascot of the Civil War, a big American bald eagle, was named "Old Abe" after him.

For three years the eagle was the fighting symbol of the Eighth Wisconsin Infantry. Once, when the company marched into camp, "Old Abe" picked up a corner of the flag and spread it out in full glory.

Wartime photograph of Old Abe

Author's collection

THE PRESIDENT TRIES
OUT A GUN . . . AUGUST 18, 1863

Mr. Lincoln and his private secretary, William O. Stoddard, went into the field behind the White House on August 18, 1863, to test guns. During the target practice, Lincoln said, "I declare, you are beating me, Stod!" Crouching, he took better aim and made seven shots in a row with the Spencer. Alarmed soldiers on guard duty in the area came on the run. Thinking some crackpots were firing near the White House, they called for the shooting to stop. They were more than surprised to find that it was the President himself who was doing the shooting.

Photograph of the pine board used for the target. Bullet holes made by Lincoln, 7 shots from a Spencer repeating rifle at 40 yards.

*The Saturday Evening Post
and J. O. Buckeridge*

Stuntz toy shop

Columbia Historical Society

A TOY FOR TAD . . . 1863

Lincoln was more affectionate than ever toward little Tad after his older brother Willie died in 1862. The President often took his boy by the hand and walked over to Joseph Stuntz's toy shop on New York Avenue, not far from the White House. In this enchanting toyland, the Civil War was forgotten while the little boy's delight refreshed his father's weary soul.

LINCOLN UTTERS IMMORTAL WORDS
AT GETTYSBURG, NOVEMBER 19, 1863

At the ceremony dedicating a national cemetery at Gettysburg, a vast crowd waited respectfully for the tall, gaunt President to speak. Edward Everett, the famous orator, had just spoken for two hours. There were many young people in the vast crowd, including a nineteen-year-old student, Henry Jacobs, who was standing in front of the speaker's stand. Young Jacobs said:

"At first his voice sounded a little strained and high-pitched, as if he were trying to throw his voice to the outer edge of the crowd. He held in his right hand the manuscript he had brought from the White House. . . . He emphasized the words 'of,' 'by,' and 'for' [the people] with a stiff yet sweeping bend of his body, holding the manuscript rigidly in both hands . . . then he drew himself up to his immense height, with his arms outstretched, as he impressively uttered the final words, 'shall not—perish—from—the earth.' "

A close-up study of the President delivering the address

130

Four score and seven years ago our fathers brought forth upon this continent, a new nation, conceived in Liberty, and dedicated to the proposition that all men are created equal.

Now we are engaged in a great civil war, testing whether that nation, or any nation so conceived, and so dedicated, can long endure. We are met on a great battle-field of that war. We have come to dedicate a portion of that field, as a final resting place for those who here gave their lives, that that nation might live. It is altogether fitting and proper that we should do this.

But, in a larger sense, we can not dedicate— we can not consecrate— we can not hallow— this ground. The brave men, living and dead, who struggled here, have consecrated it, far above our poor power to add or detract. The world will little note, nor long remember, what we say here, but it can never forget what they did here. It is for us the living, rather, to be dedicated here to the unfinished work which they who fought here, have, thus far, so nobly advanced. It is rather for us to be here dedicated to the great task remaining before us— that from these honored dead we take increased devotion to that cause for which they here gave the last full measure of devotion— that we here highly resolve that these dead shall not have died in vain— that this nation, under God, shall have a new birth of freedom— and that, government of the people, by the people, for the people, shall not perish from the earth.

THE GETTYSBURG ADDRESS IN THE HANDWRITING OF ABRAHAM LINCOLN

THE GETTYSBURG ADDRESS AS PRESIDENT LINCOLN WROTE IT . . . 1863

This copy of the famous speech Lincoln made at Gettysburg was written at the request of Edward Everett, who had made the main address that day. In 1944 the school children of Illinois helped to buy the original copy, and gave it to the Illinois State Historical Library, where it can be seen today.

LINCOLN'S ARTIST . . . 1864

On several occasions artist Frank B. Carpenter, who lived at the White House for six months, went to Brady's photograph gallery with President Lincoln. There Carpenter had photographs made of Lincoln, the principal subject of the large painting he was doing. He worked from these likenesses at times when the President could not sit for him. Lincoln sat on February 10, and again on February 12, 1864—the second time on his fifty-fifth birthday.

At least three photographs were taken "in the attitude I have designed for him," wrote Carpenter in his diary. One splendid plate, broken on the edges, was kept by the artists' grandson, Emerson Carpenter Ives. Long unpublished, it was presented by Ives to the author in 1956.

Lincoln's Secretary of State, William H. Seward, confided to a friend that "Mr. Lincoln talked to no one so freely as Mr. Carpenter."

Emerson Carpenter Ives

Frank B. Carpenter's painting, "The Reading of the Emancipation Proclamation," as Lincoln saw it, before overpainting was done on it in later years

LINCOLN AND CARPENTER'S CHILDREN . . .

MAY, 1864

When artist Frank Carpenter spent six months in the White House in 1864 to paint his famous canvas, "The Reading of the Emancipation Proclamation," the President often dropped into his studio to see the work.

Little Herbert "Bertie" Carpenter and his older sister Florence became his fast friends—an example of the President's fondness for youngsters.

133

A TALL TARGET FOR THE ENEMY...
JULY 11 AND 12, 1864

At Fort Stevens, President Lincoln witnessed Confederate General Jubal Early's attack which got as far as the outskirts of Washington. A soldier roughly ordered him off the parapet for his own safety. The next day, he again saw the soldiers turn back the raiders, and while he watched, an officer at his side was killed. Another young officer, Oliver Wendell Holmes, Jr., shouted: "Get down, you fool!" Finally General Horatio Wright persuaded the Chief Executive to stop being an eye-witness as well as a target. Lincoln remains the only man who, while President, faced enemy guns.

Author's collection

G. D. Wakely's photograph of President Lincoln's summer residence

A SCENE THAT STUCK IN A
BOY'S MEMORY . . . SEPTEMBER, 1864

During the summer months, young Anton Heitmuller often paused while playing in his front yard to watch President Lincoln pass up Fourteenth Street to the Soldier's Home, Lincoln's summer residence. He was often followed by a three-legged dog, and a cavalry escort in the rear.

135

LINCOLN AND THE YOUNG SCULPTRESS . . .
DECEMBER, 1864

An eighteen-year-old girl, Vinnie Ream, sculptured President Lincoln's bust from life. She had been an assistant to the famous Washington sculptor, Clark Mills. During the winter months of 1864 and 1865, the President gave her a number of half-hour sittings at the White House.

The old photograph shows her completed work.

Author's collection

ABRAHAM LINCOLN.
BY VINNIE REAM.

A CHRISTMAS GIFT FOR A SOUTHERN MISS...

DECEMBER 25, 1864

Laura Jones, a twenty-three-year-old girl, wanted a pass to Richmond, Virginia, where she planned to be married. The Southern beauty was a good friend of the wife of Gideon Welles, Secretary of the Navy. As a Cabinet minister, Welles used his influence with Lincoln to see that she received her pass.

Mr. Welles placed a formal request in writing on the President's desk, briefly mentioned the girl's plight, and as he left the office, purposely did not close the door. Such requests were usually granted if the person took the oath of allegiance, but Welles knew this stubborn girl would not take the oath; she claimed her only allegiance to Virginia. However, Welles was also aware of Lincoln's belief—"that you can tell a great deal by a person's face"—and hoped Lincoln would see her.

Lincoln did see her. The young lady smiled as the President looked up from his papers, and Lincoln pushed the paper aside and wrote out a pass for her.

137

THE WHITE HOUSE DURING LINCOLN'S OCCUPANCY . . . 1861–1865

While on the White House grounds the President did not always dress as formally as one might expect. One Ohio soldier, Private William L. Stokley, who was on guard duty in the area, was asked by General Winfield Hancock to take a message to the President. While walking through the grounds trying to find the right entrance to the White House, Stokley met a tall, slender man near the barn and asked where he might find President Lincoln. The tall man replied, "I'm Lincoln." "Oh, good Lord!" exclaimed the private. "I thought you were the hostler!"

South front, White House, 1864, showing flagpole and bandstand

Author's collection

North front, White House, 1863

138

Library of Congress

THE WAR-BURDENED PRESIDENT OFTEN
WALKED ALONE . . . 1861–1865

The tall, familiar figure of Abraham Lincoln was often seen alone around the streets and buildings in Washington as he attended to his weighty business; sometimes the public did not even recognize him.

The Capitol dome was completed by 1865. A soldier stands by the iron fence in this wartime photograph.

Mrs. Albert C. Heyser

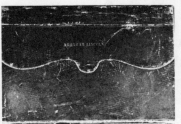

Photograph of Lincoln's leather briefcase, courtesy of Mrs. Albert C. Heyser, who received it from Mrs. Robert T. Lincoln as a gift

139

Author's collection

LINCOLN'S
SECOND INAUGURAL . . .
MARCH 4, 1865

". . . With malice toward none; with charity for all; with firmness in the right, as God gives us to see the right, let us strive on to finish the work we are in . . ."

As President Lincoln spoke these words of his second inaugural address, the motion of his body caused a blur in the photograph. This rare picture, recently discovered, also reveals many other known people in the crowd; assassin-to-be John Wilkes Booth (*under arrow*) looks on from above.

The drawing gives us a close view of the Chief Executive, wearing spectacles as he reads his famous and prayerful address.

CONFERENCE ABOARD THE "RIVER QUEEN" . . . 1865

On this comfortable steamer, the *River Queen*, President Lincoln and Secretary of State William H. Seward held the famous conference at Hampton Roads as they met February 3, 1865, with the Southern leaders, Vice-President Alexander H. Stephens, Judge John A. Campbell, and Robert M. T. Hunter.

The saloon room of the *River Queen* was also the scene of a meeting between President Lincoln, Generals Ulysses S. Grant and William T. Sherman, and Admiral David D. Porter. Here, on March 27 and 28, 1865, the final strategy of the Civil War was mapped out.

LINCOLN AND GRANT CONFER AT
PETERSBURG . . . 1865

When Petersburg, Virginia, was evacuated, General Grant sent a message to President Lincoln, inviting him to come to his headquarters, a private house in the town. So, along with Tad, Lincoln went to Hancock Station, where he met his eldest son, Captain Robert Lincoln of Grant's staff.

For an hour and a half the top Union general and his Commander-in-Chief talked. That same evening Richmond was evacuated. The President had been on the scene, an actual eyewitness to the closing days of the Civil War, having spent a total of sixteen days at the front with the Army and Navy leaders.

LINCOLN ADMIRES
A GREAT TREE
IN PETERSBURG . . . 1865

With Lincoln during the closing
days of the Civil War was the
Marquis de Chambrun, an un-
official ambassador from France.
The Marquis told how, one day
when they were walking in
Petersburg, Virginia, Lincoln
paused to comment on a very tall
and beautiful tree they passed, a
tree that reminded him of the
great oaks and beeches of his
youth. He compared the different
types of trees in detail, revealing
an extraordinary knowledge of
nature.

143

The Wilmer McLean house in
Appomattox, Virginia, where
General Robert E. Lee surren-
dered to General Ulysses S.
Grant

APPOMATTOX, SCENE OF SURRENDER . . .
APRIL 9, 1865

In mud-splattered uniform, Grant made his way into the house and
room in Appomattox where General Lee, in new uniform, was waiting
for him. Their greeting was polite, and they soon began to talk about
their former acquaintance. Then the terms were stated, written out,
and signed, bringing a long and painful war to an end. Grant, following Lincoln's advice, allowed the Southern soldiers to keep their horses
and side arms.

General Ulysses S. Grant, by the famous photographer, Mathew B. Brady, in 1865

General Robert E. Lee, by the Richmond photographer, Julian Vannerson, 1865

This rare photograph shows a Union soldier with a group of South Carolina slaves who had been given their freedom in 1865.

WAR-RAVAGED RICHMOND IN 1865—
AS LINCOLN SAW IT . . .
APRIL 4 AND 5, 1865

(*Top photo*) Wartime photograph showing view of Butchertown as seen from Jefferson Davis's Mansion at Richmond, Virginia. Shockoe Creek and the Confederate camp are in the background.

(*lower photo*) President Lincoln and his party saw Richmond in ruins, as revealed in this striking photograph, which has never been published before.

L. M. U. collection

L. M. U. collection

This old photograph of the time shows President Jefferson Davis's abandoned mansion in Richmond.

A VISIT TO THE RICHMOND RESIDENCE OF
JEFFERSON DAVIS . . . 1865

President Lincoln and a small party traveled by steamboat up the James River to Richmond on April 4, 1865. Lincoln, his son Tad, and their escort went on foot through the war-torn city until they reached the abandoned mansion of President Jefferson Davis. In a room used as an office, Lincoln sat down and remarked, "This must have been President Davis's chair."

147

ONE OF TAD LINCOLN'S PRANKS . . . 1865

Tad Lincoln playfully waved a Confederate flag from
the window of the White House as the returning
Union troops paraded in worn uniforms and tattered
bunting. Old Edward, a servant, tried vainly to stop
the display, but the crowds, as well as President Lincoln, viewed the incident good-naturedly.

THE BAND PLAYED "DIXIE" . . . 1865

The terrible war was over.

On April 10, 1865, crowds gathered on the White House lawn, making cheerful demonstrations and calling for the President. Lincoln finally appeared and gave his last informal talk, stating that once again the people were all countrymen. Smiling to the band leader, he said, "I have always thought 'Dixie' one of the best tunes I have ever heard. . . . I now request the band to favor me with its performance."

Old photograph of the Ford's Theatre stage and the Presidential flag-draped box. The original enlarged picture was presented by Edwin M. Stanton's grandson to the Illinois State Historical Library.

THE SCENE AND RELICS OF A NATIONAL TRAGEDY...
APRIL 14, 1865

The Playbill for April 14, 1865— Good Friday—announcing the cast appearing at Ford's Theatre for the fateful evening performance

The rocking chair used by Lincoln the night he was shot

Photograph of the actual derringer and lead bullet used by Booth to kill President Lincoln

150

LINCOLN'S LAST CONSCIOUS MOMENTS . . .

APRIL 14, 1865

At Ford's Theatre in Washington that fateful night of April 14, 1865, was one eyewitness, John Deering, Jr., a Treasury Department employee, who wrote about the event:

"The acting was excellent . . . the President and Mrs. Lincoln seemed to enjoy it highly—the latter in particular. . . . I could detect a broad smile on Uncle Abraham's face very often, while at other times he rested his face in both hands, bending forward, seemingly buried in deep thought. . . ."

151

ENTER, EXIT, JOHN WILKES BOOTH ...
APRIL 14, 1865

The dreadful deed was done. The mortally wounded President slumped forward as actor John Wilkes Booth played his last, most daring role in the theater. Jumping from Lincoln's box, after shooting the President, and stabbing a young officer seated with Lincoln, he caught his spur on the draped flag and landed on the stage off balance, breaking the shinbone in his left leg. Painfully recovering, he shouted, "Sic Semper Tyrannis" (Thus ever to tyrants), and made his exit quickly, before the audience fully realized what had happened.

The handsome assassin believed that his mad act had avenged the South; actually the Confederacy lost its best chance for an easier reconstruction after the war.

AT LINCOLN'S BEDSIDE
WHEN HE DIED . . .
APRIL 15, 1865

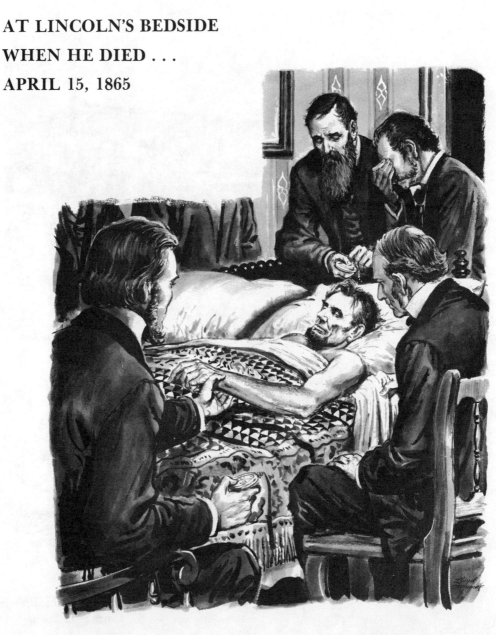

After Lincoln was fatally wounded, his limp body was carried across the street to the Peterson Boardinghouse. There the President's long body was laid on a bed and his clothing removed so the doctors could look for other wounds beside the fatal bullet hole in his head.

For nine hours Lincoln lay dying. Friends and family watched and grieved, but nothing could be done for him. Everyone waited tearfully through the night, until the first streaks of dawn lit the somber room. Death came at 7:22 that morning.

This photo by Carbutt shows Lincoln's funeral train engine, No. 57, Chicago to Springfield.

THEY WATCHED FOR THE TRAIN . . .

APRIL, MAY, 1865

Slowly the Lincoln funeral train made its way from Washington, D.C., to Springfield, Illinois.

Day and night, town after town, the mourning people anxiously waited, stared, scattered flowers, built bonfires.

This photo by Norton and Luther shows the funeral train at Cleveland, Ohio.

SILENTLY, SADLY, THEY WATCHED IT GO . . .
APRIL, MAY, 1865

Flags were draped and bands played dirges while guns were fired and church bells tolled, showing the overwhelming heartbreak of a nation that, weeping, was taking part in the largest display of grief the country had ever seen.

155

THE LINCOLN MEMORIAL,
WASHINGTON, D. C. . . . TODAY

The Lincoln Memorial, the work of architect Henry Bacon, from a photograph taken soon after it was completed in 1923. This timeless structure of beauty and vitality is a fit tribute to Lincoln.

Daniel Chester French was the sculptor who designed the heroic Lincoln statue within the memorial. The 22-foot, 8-inch high Georgia-marble likeness was carved by the Piccirilli brothers.

IN THIS TEMPLE
AS IN THE HEARTS OF THE PEOPLE
FOR WHOM HE SAVED THE UNION
THE MEMORY OF ABRAHAM LINCOLN
IS ENSHRINED FOREVER

THE LINCOLN
MONUMENT AND TOMB
AT SPRINGFIELD . . . TODAY

The Lincoln Tomb, from a photograph taken in 1883 by John Carroll Power, the first custodian. The structure at Oak Ridge Cemetery was begun in 1869 and finished in 1874.

This graceful memorial, built of Quincy granite and measuring 117 feet high, was designed and erected by Larkin G. Mead, Jr., who also modeled the Lincoln statue and figure groupings, which were cast in bronze.

Now Lincoln belongs to the ages.

157

ACKNOWLEDGMENTS

The inspiration for this picture book developed gradually, beginning with a boyhood fascination for the unusual face of Abraham Lincoln. As a youth I was intrigued by the mystic quality, profound dignity, and nobly balanced features I saw in pictures of this rugged-faced American, and ever since I have ardently pursued an avocation of painting and studying the portraits of this great man. As I am an artist by profession, and have a high regard for telling stories in pictures, completing the over 150 illustrations for this book was a labor of love, often competing with my commercial art business for time and attention.

My primary obligation is to the publishers for their enthusiasm, and for giving me the opportunity to realize my long-felt desire to write and illustrate a Lincoln book. Philip Van Doren Stern first suggested to them the idea for a Lincoln picture book to appeal to younger readers, and the editors received it warmly.

Here is an attempt to portray realistically some of the interesting highlights in the life of Lincoln. With the use of rare, old, or documentary photographs of the people, places, and relics of Lincoln's day, combined with drawings to enhance and authenticate the illustrations, a new approach, I hope, has been achieved in pictorial biography.

Besides the author's own Lincoln collection, many libraries, historical societies, and Lincoln experts have contributed advice, pictures, and material to this volume. Generous help came from the staff of the Illinois State Historical Library, particularly from Clyde C. Walton, historian; Margaret A. Flint, assistant state historian; and the ever helpful James T. Hickey, curator of the Lincoln collection. The Chicago Historical Society was especially helpful with pictures from their files.

The vast picture collections in the Library of Congress and that of the National Archives were drawn upon. My thanks to Hirst Milhollen, Virginia Daiker, and Josephine Cobb for their valuable assistance.

For years my frequent visits to the Lincoln National Life Foundation at Fort Wayne, Indiana, have been a source of inspiration. Director Emeritus Louis A. Warren and R. Gerald McMurtry, the present director, have long given encouragement and aid to this Lincoln student.

Generous assistance came from Wayne C. Temple, director of the Department of Lincolniana at Lincoln Memorial University, Harrogate, Tennessee. As editor of the *Lincoln Herald* he has published a number of my Lincoln drawings, some of which were selected for reproduction herein. I am also grateful to him for checking my facts.

Other individuals have found ways to be helpful. I owe a debt of gratitude to two Lincoln devotees in Indiana, Ora V. Brown of Dale and Adah L. Sutton of Attica.

For kind editorial assistance in the preparation of the picture captions I am grateful to Philip Van Doren Stern.

I cannot forget to thank my capable art teachers, who years ago helped me to become an artist. Many of them almost despaired of my learning to draw people, maintaining that "Everybody I drew looked like Lincoln." Foremost among my instructors and those who took special interest in my art career were Martha K. Schauer, Edward R. Burroughs, John King, Robert C. Koepnick, and Milton Caniff.

A special thanks to the following publishing firms for permission to reprint several illustrations: the George A. Pflaum Publishing Company, with whom I have long been associated, for permission to reproduce eight illustrations from their periodicals; the Dayton *Daily News* for pieces of art that appeared in their magazine, *Camerica*.

LLOYD OSTENDORF

Dayton, Ohio
October, 1961

KENTUCKY

1. John James Audubon State Park, Henderson. Bird sanctuary. Museum. Nature Center. Recreation facilities.
2. Lincoln Heritage House, Elizabethtown. Built by Thomas Lincoln before Abraham's birth.
3. Abraham Lincoln Birthplace National Historic Site, Hodgenville. Located on Sinking Spring Farm site. Visitors Center. Interpretative film.
4. Lincoln's Boyhood Home, Knob Creek. Reconstructed cabin where Abraham lived from age two to seven. Gift Shop.
5. My Old Kentucky Home State Park, Bardstown. Guided tours through Federal Hill. Camping. Picnic area. Golf.
6. Lincoln Homestead State Park, Springfield. Reconstructed cabins, blacksmith shop. Nancy Hanks' girlhood home. Golf.
7. Perryville Battlefield State Shrine, Perryville. Civil War battlefield. Museum and diorama. Picnic area.
8. Old Fort Harrod State Park, Harrodsburg. First permanent pioneer settlement west of Allegheny Mountains. Lincoln Marriage Temple. Museum. Pioneer cemetery.
9. Shakertown at Pleasant Hill, near Harrodsburg. Restored 19th-century Shaker village. Guided tours. Inn. Museum. Dining Room. Gift Shop.
10. Waveland State Shrine, near Lexington. Restored estate of Daniel Boone's great-nephew. Kentucky Life Museum.
11. Kentucky State Capitol, Frankfort. Also in Frankfort: Old State Capitol. Historical Museum. Zoo.
12. Farmington, Louisville. Guided tour of home built from Jefferson design. Also in Louisville: Culbertson Mansion, Brennan House, Locust Grove, Churchill Downs Race Track & Museum. Kentucky Railway Museum. Zoo. Belle of Louisville. Bernheim Forest. Recreation facilities.
13. Constitution Square State Shrine, Danville. Square where Kentucky statehood was born. Reconstructed buildings.
14. Lake Cumberland State Resort Park, near Jamestown. Lodge. Golf. Water-oriented recreation.
15. Mammoth Cave National Park, Mammoth Cave. Tours. Lodging. Campground.
16. Beech Bend Park, near Bowling Green. Camping. Outdoor recreation. Auto racing.
17. Jefferson Davis Monument State Shrine, Fairview. Elevator to top of 351-ft. tower commemorating President of Confederacy. Picnic area. Playground.

INDIANA

18. George Rogers Clark National Memorial, Vincennes, honoring Revolutionary War hero. Interpretative program. Also in Vincennes: Old Cathedral Complex. First Capitol of Indiana Territory. Elihu Stout Print Shop. Grouseland, home of President William Henry Harrison.
19. Indiana State Capitol, Indianapolis. Also in Indianapolis: 500 Mile Speedway & Museum. Indianapolis Museum of Art. Children's Museum. James Whitcomb Riley Home. Indianapolis Zoo. Fort Benjamin Harrison. Indiana Repertory Theatre. Conner Prairie Pioneer Village. Museum of Indian Heritage.
20. Angel Mounds Historical Memorial, Evansville. Mound-building Indian excavation and displays. Also in Evansville: Museum of Arts and Science. Mesker Amusement Park and Zoo.
21. Historic New Harmony, New Harmony. Restored community that was scene of two early-1800's communal experiments. Roofless Church. Paul Tillich Park. Inn. Restaurant. Harmonie State Recreation Area with campsites.
22. Lincoln Boyhood National Memorial and State Park, Lincoln City. Visitors Center. Interpretative program. Living farm. Nancy Hanks' grave.
23. Lincoln Museum, Fort Wayne. Collection of original Lincoln photographs; over 10,000 Lincoln books.
24. First State Capitol, Corydon. Circa 1810; site of first Indiana Constitutional Convention. Battleground memorabilia.
25. Lincoln Pioneer Village, Rockport. Reconstructed 1800's village.
26. Santa Claus Land, Santa Claus. Christmas year 'round. Restaurant. Gift shop. Recreation. Golf. Amusement Park for children.
27. Howard National Steamboat Museum, Jeffersonville. Victorian mansion filled with steamboat era memorabilia.
28. Lincoln Hills Country — Troy, Tell City, Cannelton, Tobinsport. Scenic drive. Wyandotte Caves; guided tours. Picnic area. Marengo Cave Park; guided cave tours.
29. Squire Boone Caverns, near Corydon. Cave discovered by Daniel Boone's brother, Squire. Art and Craft Shop. Camping. Picnic groves.
30. Brown County State Park, near Nashville. Scenic area. Wildlife exhibits. Nature Center. Campground. Outdoor recreation. Art Colony and Shopper's Lane in Nashville.
31. McCormick's Creek State Park, Spencer. Hiking. Horseback riding. Camping. Nature Center. Swimming.
32. Spring Mill State Park, Mitchell. Reconstructed pioneer village. Virgil I. Grissom Memorial. Camping. Inn. Nature preserve.

ILLINOIS

33. Lincoln Trail Monument, near Lawrenceville. Marks spot where Thomas Lincoln family crossed Wabash River to make their home in Illinois.
34. Lincoln Trail State Park, near Marshall. Picnic facilities. Hiking. Water-oriented recreation.
35. Lincoln Log Cabin State Park, near Charleston/Mattoon. Replica of cabin where Lincoln's father and stepmother spent final days. Living farm. Interpretative program. Picnic area.
36. Lincoln Trail Homestead State Park, near Decatur. Lincoln's first Illinois home reconstructed. Picnic area. Hiking. Water sports.
37. Mount Pulaski Courthouse, Mount Pulaski. One of two original courthouses on the 8th judicial circuit traveled by Abraham Lincoln as a young lawyer.
38. Postville Courthouse, Lincoln. Reconstructed courthouse on 8th judicial circuit. Also in Lincoln: Lincoln College Museum. Lincoln Savings Gallery.
39. Long Nine Museum, Athens. Commemorates success of Lincoln and eight associates in moving Illinois' capital from Vandalia to Springfield.
40. Lincoln's New Salem State Park, near Petersburg. Reconstructed New Salem village where Lincoln spent six years. Interpretative program. Summer outdoor drama "Your Obedient Servant, A. Lincoln". Camping. Picnic area. Hiking. Gift Shop. Lodge nearby. Also in Petersburg: New Salem Carriage Museum. Illinois. Country Opry. Gay 90's Museum. Saddle Tramp Gap. Edgar Lee Masters' home.
41. Clayville Rural Life Center, Pleasant Plains. Restored stagecoach stop. Museum of rural life. Pioneer Craft Shop. Country Kitchen Restaurant. Summer craft festivals.
42. Springfield ... Concentration of Lincoln sites. Lincoln's Home. Lincoln's Tomb. Restored Old State Capitol, site of "House Divided" speech; "Sound & Light Show" nightly during summer. Abraham Lincoln Museum. Ninian Edwards Home. Lincoln Railroad Depot. Lincoln/Herndon Law Office. Illinois State Capitol. Illinois State Museum. Oliver P. Parks Telephone Museum. Guided tours and interpretative programs.
43. Vandalia Statehouse, Vandalia. Illinois' capitol from 1820-1839 where Lincoln headed "Long Nine", legislators influential in moving capital to Springfield.
44. Carl Sandburg Birthplace, Galesburg. Museum. Near Galesburg: Bishop Hill, restored Swedish Colony.
45. Nauvoo Historic Mormon Settlement, Nauvoo. 1840 vintage village; more than a dozen restored Mormon homes, stores and offices, including homes of Brigham Young and Joseph Smith. Interpretative program. Picnic area. Hiking. Outdoor recreation.
46. Lincoln Memorial Park, downtown Mt. Carmel. Public Library/Museum. Beall Woods State Park with the largest tract of virgin forest in U.S.A. Red Barn nature center.

Map of above-listed historic points of interest shown on back cover.